Beluga Whales

Leo Statts

abdopublishing.com

Published by Abdo Zoom™, PO Box 398166, Minneapolis, Minnesota 55439. Copyright © 2017 by Abdo Consulting Group, Inc. International copyrights reserved in all countries. No part of this book may be reproduced in any form without written permission from the publisher. Abdo Zoom™ is a trademark and logo of Abdo Consulting Group, Inc.

Printed in the United States of America, North Mankato, Minnesota
062016
092016

THIS BOOK CONTAINS
RECYCLED MATERIALS

Cover Photo: Luna Vandoorne/Shutterstock Images, cover
Interior Photos: iStockphoto, 1, 4–5, 12–13, 15 (bottom); Tyson Paul/iStockphoto, 6; Shutterstock Images, 7; Christopher Meder/Shutterstock Images, 9; CampCrazy Photography/Shutterstock Images, 10, 11, 18–19; Red Line Editorial, 13, 20 (left), 20 (right), 21 (left), 21 (right); Stanislav Komogorov/iStockphoto, 14; Feng Yu/iStockphoto, 15 (top); John Wollwerth/Shutterstock Images, 17

Editor: Emily Temple
Series Designer: Madeline Berger
Art Direction: Dorothy Toth

Publisher's Cataloging-in-Publication Data
Names: Statts, Leo, author.
Title: Beluga whales / by Leo Statts.
Description: Minneapolis, MN : Abdo Zoom, [2017] | Series: Polar animals |
    Includes bibliographical references and index.
Identifiers: LCCN 2016941138 | ISBN 9781680791860 (lib. bdg.) |
    ISBN 9781680793543 (ebook) | ISBN 9781680794434 (Read-to-me ebook)
Subjects: LCSH: White whale--Juvenile literature.
Classification: DDC 599.5--dc23
LC record available at http://lccn.loc.gov/2016941138

Table of Contents

Beluga Whales

Beluga whales are also called white whales. *Beluga* means "white" in Russian.

Belugas are noisy.

They make loud whistles.
The whales use these noises
to **communicate**.

Body

Adult beluga whales
are mostly white. They have
a thick layer of **blubber**.
Their bodies are rounded.

They have small **flippers**.

Each whale has a **melon**.
It is a bump on the head.

Habitat

Belugas live in northern areas. They are in the Arctic Ocean. Sometimes they are in rivers.

Where belugas live

Food

Beluga whales eat fish.

They eat crabs.

They even eat octopuses.

Belugas hunt their **prey**.
They dive deep underwater.

Life Cycle

Belugas have one baby at a time. The baby is called a calf.

Calves stay with their mothers for two years. Belugas can live for more than 50 years.

Average Length

A male beluga whale is shorter than a midsize car.

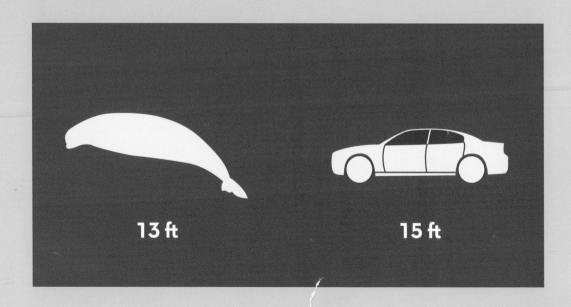

13 ft   15 ft

Average Weight

A male beluga whale weighs as much as three soda vending machines.

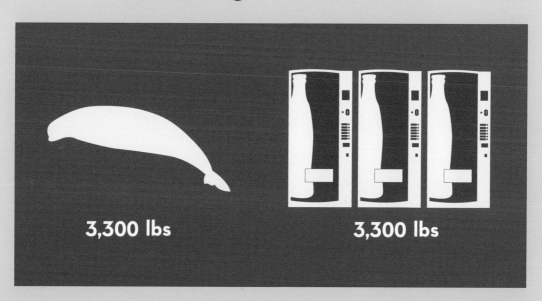

3,300 lbs   3,300 lbs

Glossary

blubber - the fat of whales and other marine mammals. Blubber protects animals from the cold.

communicate - to give and receive information.

flippers - wide, flat limbs sea creatures use for swimming.

melon - a rounded structure found in the forehead of some whales.

prey - an animal hunted or killed by a predator for food.

Booklinks

For more information on
beluga whales, please visit
booklinks.abdopublishing.com

Zꟾm In on Animals!

Learn even more with the Abdo Zoom
Animals database. Check out
abdozoom.com for more information.

Index

24